WHY SCOUTING WORKS FOR BLACK BOYS

JUSTIN LEWTER

Chicago, Illinois

First Edition, First Printing

Front cover illustration by Harold Carr

Printed in the United States of America

10-Digit ISBN #: 1-934155-07-3
13-Digit ISBN #: 978-1-934155-10-3

CONTENTS

ACKNOWLEDGMENTS

I can't say enough about Jerome A. Goode, Robert Purvis, Doug Thorne, Nelson Rankin, Gem Jones, and volunteer and professional leaders seriously committed to helping all boys grow into great men. Each in his own way has and continues to positively influence Scouts and Scouters alike. For me, they have symbolized what is best about scouting.

I take my hat off to all volunteer leaders, professional and paraprofessional staff who work in underprivileged communities, and also to any and all who have contributed directly or indirectly to the success of Scouting programs in our communities. This is exactly what Lord Baden Powell, founder of the Boy Scout movement, envisioned.

Why Scouting Works For Black Boys

Introduction

Our children encounter a pandemic of social, economic, and psychological horrors that put them into the equivalent of a deep dark hole. This hole is difficult to climb out of in and of itself, while the social backlash in the form of the criminal justice system and law enforcement act as grave diggers, tossing dirt down on every child attempting to climb out. This condition is further compounded by the many hands at the bottom of this pit that clutch, pull, and claw desperately at the heels of every child who has the desire and determination to reach the light above.

What to do about it? The first and easiest step is to give this book serious consideration. As this book addresses primarily the state of black boys in America, it's obviously not the only solution. It may not even be the best. But you will find in this book, unlike many others on this topic, the basic elements that are fundamental to changing the fate of African American boys in America.

What you will not find here is a book of theory, a mere diatribe on the conditions with no discussion or outline of action(s) to be taken to improve and change these conditions. We have no time for that. I don't believe you will find any great wisdom or deep truth other than the fact that this program works. It works when interested adults commit and act to change a young person's life, thereby changing the life of our community.

The worst thing we can choose to do as adults, as men in particular, is nothing. If we recognize and acknowledge that our children are in dire straits, we are compelled to act. At least we should be. Unfortunately, many men are still boys. Confounded by material toys and selfish desires, they don't realize the real power they wield in the community and in the lives of the young men who see them every day.

Even those of us who are aware of our potential to influence youth must move past just taking care of "me and mine." "Family" must extend to the neighborhood and the community, eventually the entire human community.

This book focuses primarily on the Boy Scout troop. The Boy Scouts is the original program established by Lord Baden Powell in 1907. The Boy Scouts of America, which was established in 1910, has developed additional programs, most notably Cub Scouting1 for boys ages 7-10 and Venturing2 for youth ages 14-20, to expand efforts to touch the lives of youth. While all these programs are effective in developing youth into concerned and capable citizens, Boy Scouting, in many ways, best exemplifies the benefits of a value-based youth development program.

1. Cub Scouting was established in 1930 as a value-based program that is age- and grade-appropriate for younger boys.
2. Venturing was established in 1998 with an emphasis on high adventure activities and as a positive alternative for teenaged boys and girls.

Boys learn skills that build confidence and teach the need for resourcefulness.

WHAT IS SCOUTING?

Let's take the opening words from the first Boy Scout Handbook published more than 90 years ago to zero in on the Scouting program's original concept and intention. In the opening paragraph the book states, under "Aim of Scout Movement":

"...It is not the aim to set up a new organization to parallel in its purposes others already established. The opportunity is afforded these organizations, however, to introduce into their programs unique features appealing to interests that are universal among boys. The method is summed up in the term Scoutcraft, and is a combination of observation, deduction, and handiness or the ability to do things.... This is accomplished in game and team play, and is pleasure, not work, for the boy. All that is needed is the out-of-doors, a group of boys, and a competent leader." (Boy Scout Handbook, 1st edition, 1911)

Scoutcraft was established to hone the physical ability and mental acuity of boys, using the outdoors and skilled leaders. Its purpose is to give youth-serving agencies a program to make boys confident, competent, and independent. This is done in the same way and with the same intention that a community might seek to prepare its sons for manhood.

What Is Scouting?

Scouting is essentially the basic body of methods used by people for thousands of years to teach a boy how to adapt, navigate, and sustain himself in an environment despite the surrounding limitations or circumstances. Add to that, lessons on the ideas, values, mores, and folkways of a community and the results constitute the fundamental concepts that guide a boy into adulthood.

Many cultures organize these basic practices into a single method called Rites of Passage. Scouting is, indeed, a rite of passage program for the modern boy, although few might describe it that way. Typically, most see Scouting as a positive program for recreation, or simply an opportunity for boys to experience the outdoors and stay out of trouble. However, the founder of Scouting sought to do more than engage youth. He wanted to prepare boys for the rigors of manhood. Though our world has changed dramatically from then till now, it remains clear that what is learned in Scouting gives young men the confidence, ability, and sensibility to solve problems and navigate the challenges of life honorably.

To accomplish its goals, Scouting requires practice, preparation, and knowledge about the minds and personalities of the individuals it seeks to help. Scouting is about the male spirit and about the outcomes it desires to see in Scouts' daily lives. In the opening passage the Handbook goes on to describe what a Scout is and the different kinds of Scouts:

"...There have been other kinds of scouts besides war scouts and frontier scouts.... These peace scouts had to be as well prepared as any war scouts. They had to know scoutcraft. They had to know how to live in the woods, and be able to find their way anywhere without other chart or compass than the sun and stars, besides being able to interpret the meaning of the slightest signs of the forest and the foot tracks of animals and men. They had to know how to live so as to keep healthy and strong, to face any danger that came their way, and to help one another." (*Boy Scout Handbook,* 1ˢᵗ edition, 1911)

Peace Scouts were merely men. Men who farmed, raised livestock, praised and worshipped a higher power, gathered to make decisions regarding the community, and if called upon defended that community with their lives. Scoutcraft teaches the fundamental principles and requirements of manhood, of being a man. Completion of these teachings grants a boy the authority of men because he has now become one of them.

Scouting today still provides boys with the same essential training. By combining basic survival skills, the use

What Is Scouting?

of tools, and knowledge of the environment with a sense of duty and honor, boys are still being prepared for manhood today. These boys are learning the kind of knowledge and skills that will benefit them for the rest of their lives.

Scouts learn to master a variety of useful skills in the presence of positive adult leaders.

SCOUTING TODAY (WHAT THEY LEARN)

"Child research has consistently demonstrated that loving and involved fathers are beneficial to the health, education, and welfare of their children. When fathers are absent from the home or are uninvolved in the learning and developmental process, children suffer." (Greater Diversity News, *6/05*)

Much of what Scouting teaches traditionally are the values and skills fathers and men pass on to sons and boys in the community. Without those male role models, these skills are lost as well as the devotion to one's culture. While sports are an effective tool, Scouting affords many more skills and talents that are relevant to daily life in both tangible and intangible ways. Much of the skills learned in athletics are useful only for one or a few sports. They don't transfer over into everyday living the way Scouting skills do, e.g., first aid, knot tying, use of tools, etc.

Here is a sampling of what we know quality Scouting programs offer boys.

1. Scouting provides a boy with the basic skills and confidence to survive independently—to be self-sufficient.

Scouting Today (What They Learn)

2. Scouting teaches a boy how to work cooperatively with peers; how to understand what leadership means; and how to both follow and be a leader.

3. Scouting can increase a boy's awareness of his surroundings – community – environment.

4. Scouting improves a boy's handiness with tools – provides hands-on learning, skill mastery.

5. Scouting reaffirms a boy's reverence for creation and Creator.

6. Scouting encourages respect for adults – strengthens the influence of adult role models.

Too many of our sons don't learn these basic skills or character-building concepts. A lack of skills and awareness leads to low self-esteem and little confidence, which can and often does lead to discipline problems. As mentioned earlier, many of these skills and self-concepts are traditionally learned from the primary adult role model in a boy's life, his father. But the epidemic increase of black children growing up in homes without fathers has created its negative opposite. The absence of a father or primary male role model is the single most important challenge facing the black family and community today. For all the initial conditions that helped to create this crisis, it has become a self-fulfilling prophecy.

Scouting has proven to be effective in preparing boys for adulthood and warrants greater consideration from our community as a program or method to be used in broader prevention strategies focused on breaking negative social cycles. When more boys are involved in a program that requires positive adult male attention and involvement, the negative social conditions that result from absent fathers can be reduced and, in some cases, altogether eliminated. For any person or agency that works with boys and seeks to address this crisis, Boy Scouting is an excellent program to include as a tool in your prevention strategy.

The challenge to create positive change in the lives of black boys is not about battling against poverty or absentee fathers alone. The challenge in working with boys today is confronting the cumulative effects that these maledictions produce.

Scouting Today (What They Learn)

"If multiple risk factors accumulate and are not offset by compensating protective factors, healthy development is compromised." (Schorr, 1989; Werner & Smith 1992)

All children learn. It is what they learn under the influence of negative conditions that must be confronted. When there is nothing to counter the negative values boys learn about "being a man" and taking care of oneself, a destructive mindset is fostered that affirms negative social perceptions and threatens the life of the community. Gang violence, abusive attitudes toward women, a lack of accountability for behavior, a lack of a sense of responsibility toward family and community, and a diminished concern for the needs of others are just some of the character flaws that develop. (Dr. Amos Wilson discusses this at length in his book, *Black on Black Male Adolescent Violence.*)

The maladaptive social conditioning, coupled with the negative impact of poverty, broken homes, racism, and broken school compounds, leave children confused about who they are and what they are worth. These confused emotions and unanswered questions eat away at the person who bears them. Self-esteem issues develop. In many, a skewed view of the world develops to compensate for their negative self-perception. This worldview is fueled by anger, depression, and emotional trouble.

The results are obvious. Children don't take feeling bad about themselves lying down. These emotions are released in the form of rage and hatred. We need only read a newspaper or watch an evening news program reporting on urban America for proof. The damage is being done in the earliest and most formative years of a boy's life. In our effort to curb the damage that is taking place, it is important that we take time to address the development of boys and, specifically, the challenges many African American boys face.

To prepare boys for manhood requires understanding of how boys see themselves.

BOYS

"...A child who experiences risk factors such as maltreatment at home, who lives in a dangerous neighborhood, and attends a poor quality childcare setting and school is unlikely to develop in a healthy manner." (Schorr, 1989)

Youth Development

The BSA (Boy Scouts of America) used research from two organizations, the Carnegie Council on Adolescent Development and the Search Institute, to identify the conditions and "developmental assets" every child needs "to grow up into healthy, constructive adults." Using these diverse data, the "six critical elements of healthy youth development" were determined.

1. Strong personal values and character

2. A positive sense of self-worth and usefulness

3. Caring and nurturing relationships with parents, other adults, and peer

4. A desire to learn

5. Productive/creative use of time

6. Social adeptness

Further research conducted by Louis Harris & Associates for the Boy Scouts of America demonstrates that each of these important elements is addressed through… *"The Boy Scout program, structure of troop meetings, patrol meetings, advancement work, and time devoted to Scouting activities outside of meetings…."* Before we explain how these methods work, let's look at the basic desires all children have:

1. They all desire to be loved—given attention, affection, and praise.
2. They all desire to be considered valuable—appreciated, recognized, and needed.
3. They all desire to feel empowered—accomplished through education, instruction, and discipline.

Every child must be given the opportunity to give as well as receive the elements of these basic desires. If a child does not learn to reciprocate these basic elements, they either have not been communicated effectively or they have not been demonstrated adequately. The tendencies and behaviors our youth exhibit are the results of these failures.

To be loved:

Attention—Obviously all children seek the eyes, ears, and faces of others, primarily their parents/caregivers. Paying attention to a child is one of the most important demonstrations of love.

Affection—Touching, such as patting a child on the head or back; hugging; holding a child's hand are expressions of affection. With small children, platonic physical contact is an essential element in communicating love (particularly when working with groups where more than one child competes for one's attention). You can make eye contact with one child while holding another's hand or placing your hand on their shoulder. This lets the child know he is not forgotten, that in fact, he is included in the conversation.

Praise—It has been said that the sweetest sound anyone hears is the sound of their own name. Praise should often be in the form of honoring a child for being, not for accomplishing, simply for being. This does not require any particular act or behavior on the child's part. It can simply be a personal greeting – an acknowledgment of the child's individual presence in the crowd.

Boys

To be considered valuable:

Appreciation—This is an honest reflection of the contribution a child makes to a group or family or classroom. It requires genuine reflection on the part of an adult. It doesn't have to be specific or tangible. But it needs to be sincere and accurate, true to the child's personality and/or contribution.

Recognition—Children need to be applauded for their efforts as well as their accomplishments. Awards or public honoring is a must for every child.

Consideration—Every child needs to feel relevant to the larger group. Make sure each child is thoughtfully considered when decisions are made about the group. Ensure that his concerns are considered equally, as much by his peers as by the adults in the group. We can all accept decisions better when we feel our needs were at least addressed by the larger group.

To feel empowered:

Education—Each waking day is a learning experience. Children need to be given information in a way that best meets both their learning styles and their needs. Children desire to learn new things. Boys, especially, need to be able to demonstrate or replicate skills on their own to prove their mastery of concepts.

Instruction—Children want to be taught how to do things. This is a form of love. Sharing concepts with the hope that the child will eventually grasp and possibly master a particular concept is an act of love. And children know it. How teaching is offered is vital and fundamentally important to how a child will receive it.

Discipline—Children do not want to be free to do whatever they want. Children appreciate order. They will gladly trade supposed freedom for mastery of a skill or concept as long as those things offer greater promise than the syncopation of "free time." Discipline is one of the highest forms of love demonstrated. It requires that you sacrifice the "cozy" atmosphere and be confrontational at times. But it is all in the hope that the child will learn the advantage of self-imposed constraints and how they are necessary to skill/concept mastery as well as life-preservation skills in the long run.

"When a child faces negative factors at home, at school, and in the neighborhood, the negative effect of these factors is multiplied rather than simply added together, because these

Boys

conditions interact with and reinforce each other." (Werner & Smith, 1992)

When these needs are not met and the basic elements of development are not present, the outcomes are varied and destructive. As described by Amos Wilson in *Understanding Black Adolescent Male Violence,* black boys are prone to suffer from chronic anger and frustration, displaced aggression, internalization of racist attitudes, ego-defense orientation, a sense of powerlessness and fatalism, consumer orientation, and a perpetual sense of threat, vulnerability, and anxiety.

What causes these needs to go unfulfilled and the absence of developmental elements? There are many factors, including historic and contemporary racism, poverty, abuse, neglect, absentee fathers, etc. All of which further contribute to engendering in most a kind of "reactionary masculinity."

"...confusion about what it means to be a man under oppression, has moved them to accept an incomplete, distorted, self-defeating, and sometimes self-destructive definition and expression of masculinity." (Wilson, 1991)

Because of what they don't understand and can't comprehend, our children are at war with us and with themselves. You don't have to believe it; just look around you.

WHY SCOUTING WORKS FOR BLACK BOYS

We don't have the luxury of continuing to lock up black males. The punitive responses offered by the larger society, despite culpability, are explicitly antithetical to our future. There is no way around that. There is no acceptable loss of boys.

If you already work with young people, what you have read is not new to you. Perhaps you have or are aware of these factors; you may even use them in your work with youth. No program can completely eradicate the challenge. But the goal here is to convince those of you who are considering doing something, to consider Scouting. Scouting is a very good choice. Very few programs offer as much for a young boy that can positively effect his development personally and socially.

According to research, the six elements determined to be necessary in the development of boys are incorporated into the Scouting program every day. The Scouting program can work for boys in your community because the essential methods it uses have worked for thousands of years. The methods used in the Scouting program predate Scouting. The methods are ancient.

While Scouting is nearly a century old, its core practices are made up of and based on far older practices for rearing adolescent boys and girls into manhood and womanhood. Scouting is based on the very methods African men and women

Boys

traditionally used to rear their boys and girls into adulthood. Scouting is an adaptation of African rites of passage practices.

Like the Poro[1] and Sande societies of West Africa, Scouting shares fundamental practices that foster independence, maturity, and responsibility. The founder of Scouting, Lord Baden Powell, conceived of Scouting with the benefit of years of observation and interaction with the people he spent most of his military career with. It takes nothing away from the genius of Powell to acknowledge where his idea came from. Nothing is created in a vacuum, including Scouting.

1. Young men and women who live in Guinea, Sierra Leone, and Liberia enter initiation societies called Poro (for boys) and Sande (for girls) to prepare them for adulthood. Adolescent boys learn farming, hunting, tribal history, and secret knowledge; and girls are educated in farming, medicine, and childrearing. These societies are similar to other practices in the region (see Odyssey Online: AFRICA/People).

AFRICAN TRADITIONAL PRACTICES

Not only do boys master a wide variety of tools in scouting, but they learn to work with discipline and focus on the task at hand.

African Traditional Practices

"Manhood is so important to the strength, vitality, and future of the community that it cannot be left up to chance."
Reggie Singleton, Mentor/Health Educator

In scenes from the epic mini-series "Roots," Kunta Kente is hooded and taken to a remote area by his father. When his hood is removed, he finds himself standing beside other boys his age, surrounded by the adult males of their village. Introduced to them is the Kintongo. The Kintongo is the elder who leads the boys through their trials and tribulations. He is the supreme authority over the group, though other adults play important roles as well.

For the next several days and even weeks, these young men will be coached, instructed, trained, and guided into and through the doorway of manhood. When they return to their village/community they will be viewed as men. Whether they feel like men or not, their actions and/or inaction will be judged against the standards and concepts they've learned. For all intents and purposes they are men, entitled to the benefits and bound to the responsibilities every man is subject to. At the conclusion of this process, they are no longer boys. The transformation is not a physical one. It is a transformation of consciousness, of ideas about oneself, one's community, and one's relationship with the Creator.

WHY SCOUTING WORKS FOR BLACK BOYS

Every man's first responsibility is to provide for his family and in that way contribute to the economic health of the overall community. He recognizes his family to be a unit of the greater village family. Just as every family member is a unit of the whole family, a man who provides food, shelter, clothing, and other basic needs guarantees the preservation of the family for another generation or more.

To provide for one's family traditionally required hunting and farming skills and knowledge of construction. Many African boys will have learned these skills before the rites of passage begin. What they may not have learned is mastery of the environment and what it offers.

Hunting today may not be a skill of primary importance, and it is not taught in Scouting. But the concept of being prepared and able to take care of oneself in almost any circumstance is something still shared. The observation skills of a hunter, the awareness of one's surroundings and environment, attention to detail, and patience are all qualities of a hunter that are still relevant. Scouting inculcates boys with these with abilities.

Another male responsibility is reverence for the spiritual-religious tradition and ritual. Men play a vital role in teaching spiritual matters. Passing on religion, ritual, and traditions is seen as crucial to the overall well-being of any community. Without men's participation, these values will decline in influence and negatively impact all aspects of the community. A simple case in point is the correspondence of today's decline in black male church attendance and the increased risk factors in the community.

A third responsibility of men is making decisions in the best interest of the family and community. Men are required to contribute intelligently to dialogues that impact the health, wealth, and well-being of the community. These decisions include political, economic, social, and spiritual matters.

The fourth male responsibility includes protecting the community. Every man, whether farmer, hunter, or warrior, is responsible for protecting his family, home, and property and the life of the village. Through training he is taught how to defend the community and himself. But more importantly, he is taught his entire duty to community. Only part of it is defense.

Because so many of our young men and women are growing up in homes without fathers, in communities without a reciprocating sense of love and concern for their well-being, it is easy for youth to adopt values and views that are self-sustaining but destructive to the larger society. We understand that while an action appears to benefit the individual in the short term or financially, if it destroys or disregards the welfare of the community in the long term, the result is the destruction of both. Drug dealers, pimps, and street thugs are prime examples of this fact. The individuals that engage in these kinds of activities see immediate benefits and some personal gain in the short term, but eventually they face death or incarceration while their acts of murder, violence, and crime wreak havoc and destroy the community.

Self-defense and defense of family and community (which includes property, even communal property) require learning martial arts or basic fighting tactics. Defense requires the mastery of weapons, hand-to-hand combat, and most importantly, strategy. Along with the skills of conflict, men are taught the skills of conflict resolution and a philosophy of the preservation of life. Violence is ultimately destructive, especially when turned inward against home, village, or family. To prevent this, as a first resort, men are taught negotiation.

Mentors role model male responsibilities, and demonstrate that it is honorable and one's duty to place the greater whole before and above one's personal needs. Men are best defined by their willingness to put themselves second. A man must be willing to put the needs of his family and his community before his own, and most importantly, he must be willing to concede to the will of his Creator. For each of these responsibilities, a set or sets of skills are shared and must be mastered. Then it must be shown that he has the ability to adequately carry them out.

Later, in the chapter on Methods of Scouting, specific practices are correlated with these responsibilities. While the tactics employed may vary from ancient traditions, the responsibilities remain nearly the same. Determining what action translates into its moral (and intangible) equivalent is a difficult endeavor. Scouting succeeds in that endeavor.

It's worth mentioning that a key basis for the establishment of the Kwanzaa holiday was to reinforce some of the very same concepts and ideas that a traditional African community values. These values are dependent upon their transference to the youth by the elders and the larger social network of the community. If you look at the Nguzo Saba (seven principles), which is the core of the seven-day celebration of Kwanzaa, you will see these very same concepts practiced and demonstrated in the methods of Scouting, as follows:

1. Unity—Troop dynamics – Uniform
2. Self-determination—Leadership roles—Advancement program—Merit Badge sash

3. Collective work and responsibility—Patrol method—
   Outdoor code –"Leave no trace" policy—Service projects
4. Cooperative economics—Patrol method
5. Purpose—Citizenship—Character development—
   Community service—Duty to country
6. Creativity—Service projects—Conservation projects
7. Faith—Scout Oath: "Duty to God"—Scout Law: "A
   Scout Is Reverent"—Religious study—Relationships
   with faith-based institutions and communities

This is just a small sample of the ways in which Scouting values and methods parallel the principles of Kwanzaa. In the same way that Kwanzaa was designed to promote these principles within the African American community, the methods of Scouting make the principles similar to tangible tools to be shared as they were in traditional African rites-of-passage societies. These tools are used to instill the values necessary to promote healthy character development in youth and thus increase a community's sustainability as children grow into adulthood.

African Traditional Practices

Scouting spans generations and provides the much needed role models for boys.

THE AIMS OF SCOUTING

1. Develop Character

2. Develop Physical, Mental, and Emotional Fitness

3. Develop Citizenship, Sense of Community

Develop Character

This is the most important aim of any program whether it is Scouting, rites of passage, or any program that is committed to helping the development of children into adulthood, in part or entirely. Character is the intangible that is, contextually, more valuable than either the aims of total fitness or sense of community. Character contributes to and is a catalyst for the other two.

Character can be defined as: One's nature; the sum total of qualities making up an individual. Character is the expression of one's attitude and beliefs about his own experiences. A person of good character is known by his/her actions. One's actions are the result of what one believes, has been taught, and has experienced. The life lessons that he/she learns and the values the individual is taught create one's character. Signs of good character are selfless behavior, kindness, honesty, fair play, pleasant disposition, commitment, and taking responsibility.

Develop Mental, Physical, and Emotional Fitness

Every boy needs to develop his body, mind, and spiritual self. In Scouting, activities and games are constructed to promote good health. A healthy body is only as good as a healthy mind and vice versa. The rugged outdoors requires a certain minimum physical health to be able to navigate the terrain. Boys are naturally active. They require room to explore and venture beyond prescribed borders. They tend to seek the challenge of what is dangerous.

One's mind must be sharp. As beautiful as the out-of-doors can be, it is equally dangerous. Everything from weather conditions and terrain to plant and animal life needs to be studied and made familiar. Safety is crucial to the program. One of the first things taught in Scouting is safety. The use of tools and equipment needed for camping requires adherence to specific safety guidelines. Use of fire, pocket knife, hand saw, axe, and medicine requires identifying poisonous plants, animals, and insects, discerning unsafe terrain, preparing for inclement weather, and learning all the attributes a Scout needs.

Scouting does not, traditionally, make physical training a part of the weekly meeting. Although this varies from troop to troop, most Scouts get physical training in the process of another activity, i.e., backpacking, canoeing, hiking, etc. The strength of this approach is that it shows the average boy that he is capable of almost any task and that he doesn't have to be an athlete to succeed at physical feats.

Spiritual fitness for some is to be found in a church or synagogue or mosque. Others find it in a temple or on a mountaintop. Really, it's to be found within no matter where you arc. What Scouting affords (like places of worship) is an opportunity to delve within a quiet place – a sacred space. Spiritual fitness is encouraged through the observation of the natural, which is in and of itself a spiritual activity. Observation can lead to a deeper look into one's own character and an awareness of one's limits and true power. A sincere reverence for any higher power has to begin there.

When boys are brought to consider the vastness of all life, all creation, they are quieted. And the quiet is where they find their center. There are no guarantees in this endeavor. What we learn in Scouting is the interconnectedness of all life, that is to say, ecology in the broadest sense.

Develop Citizenship, Sense of Community

America cheers the rugged individualists. Our history lessons speak highly of the early explorers and their pursuits, giving them a legendary status. However, from then to now the building of our nation has never been the result of just a few but the efforts and success of a great many. The individual is useless to the community if he/she does not live for it. To live for oneself is death to both.

Citizenship is about belief-oriented action. Citizenship is the honorable behavior of an individual toward a group or idea with which he/she has a positive identification. Because of his/her identification, the individual demonstrates a sense of responsibility and appreciation by making an effort to contribute to the idea or group.

It is vital that black boys see adult males in leadership roles in the community.

METHODS OF SCOUTING

"It is easier to mold behavior than to change it."

—Unknown

The following are the basic methods used in Scouting:

1. Scout Oath—Ideals and values
2. Scout Law—Ideals and values
3. Patrols—Small groups
4. Outdoors—Being close to nature helps Scouts appreciate God, environment, and social group
5. Advancement—Self-confidence through overcoming obstacles and goal achievement
6. Adult association—Positive role modeling
7. Personal growth—Good turn daily concept—Service projects
8. Leadership development—Opportunities to learn and practice how to lead and follow
9. Uniform—Identity, recognition, positive youth image, and commitment to ideals

As stated earlier, the methods of Scouting are used to facilitate the development of character, total fitness, and

Methods of Scouting

citizenship (see correlations below) and are directly derived from traditional African practices. Such practices were used in the same way to achieve the same ends.

Character—Methods 1, 3, 6, 7

Physical, mental, emotional fitness—Methods 3, 4, 5, 6, 7

Citizenship, sense of community—Methods 1, 2, 3, 6, 8

Scouting is a great substitute for traditional rites of passage programs. Traditional programs require taking youth out of the community for a specific period of time, anywhere from five days to eight weeks or more. What that requires is a well-organized community that shares the same values and geography. Our lifestyles and living circumstances no longer make these conditions practical. But when you take the same core values and temper the methods to teach them effectively within the new circumstances, you can still achieve the original end and acquire the same result. That is what Scouting does.

The Meaning of the Scout Oath and Scout Law have been excerpted in their entirety from the *Boy Scout Handbook*, 10th edition, Chapter 24, pages 550-563. (Refer to appendix D for other components of the Scouting program.)

WHY SCOUTING WORKS FOR BLACK BOYS

1. THE MEANING OF THE SCOUT OATH

On my honor ...

By giving your word, you are promising to make every effort to live by the high ideals of the Scout Oath. Your success is a measure of your honor. As a Scout, you must hold your honor sacred.

I will do my best ...

You have many talents, skills, and interests. Do your best with them, and use them for good purposes. Don't be satisfied with less than your best effort even when less is required of you. Measure your achievements against your own high standards, not against the performance of the others. As a Scout and throughout your life, you will have opportunities to learn and to help many people. You will also be faced with challenges that may severely test you. Use your abilities to do your very best. That is what Scouting requires.

To do my duty to God ...

Your family and religious leaders teach you to know and love God and the ways in which God can be served. As a Scout, you do your duty to God by following the wisdom of those teachings in your daily life, and by respecting the rights of others to have their own religious beliefs.

and my country …

As you study our country's history, you learn about the men and women who toiled to make America great. Most contributed in quiet ways. Others sacrificed their lives for our country. All of them did their part to build the nation we have today. Help keep the United States strong by obeying its laws. Learn about our system of government and your role as a citizen and future voter. Do all you can to help your family and neighbors live happy, productive lives. The land itself is an important part of our national heritage. Work for the conservation of our natural resources. Teach others respect for the land. Your efforts really will make a difference.

and to obey the Scout Law …

The 12 points of the Scout Law are the rules of Scouting. They are also rules you can apply to your whole life. The Scout Law sets forth ideals to live up to. By using the Scout Law as a guide, you will know you are always doing your best. Others will respect you for the way you live. Most importantly, you will respect yourself.

WHY SCOUTING WORKS FOR BLACK BOYS

To help other people at all times …

There are many people who need you. Your young shoulders can help them carry their burdens. A cheerful smile and a helpful hand will make life easier for many who need assistance. By helping whenever aid is needed and by doing a Good Turn daily, you prove yourself a Scout. You are doing your part to make this a better world.

To keep myself physically strong …

Take care of your body. Protect it and develop it so that it will serve you well for an entire lifetime. That means eating nutritious foods and being active to build strength and endurance. It also means avoiding drugs, alcohol, tobacco, and any other practices that can destroy your health.

mentally awake …

Develop your mind. Strive to increase your knowledge and make the greatest use of your abilities. Be curious about the world around you. Learn all you can both in class and beyond school. With an open attitude and the willingness to ask questions, you will get the most out of your life.

Methods of Scouting

and morally straight...

To be a person of strong character, guide your life with honesty, purity, and justice. Respect and defend the rights of all people. Your relationships with others should be honest and open. Be clean in your speech and actions, and faithful in your religious beliefs. The values you follow as a Scout will help you become virtuous and self-reliant.

2. SCOUT LAW

Each Law is followed by its meaning .

A Scout is TRUSTWORTHY. A Scout tells the truth. He keeps his promises. Honesty is a part of his code of conduct. People can always depend on him.

A Scout is LOYAL. A Scout is true to his family, friends, Scout leaders, school, nation, and world community.

A Scout is HELPFUL. A Scout is concerned about other people. He willingly volunteers to help others without expecting payment or reward.

A Scout is FRIENDLY. A Scout is a friend to all. He is a brother to other Scouts and all the people of the world. He seeks to understand others. He respects those with ideas and customs that are different from his own.

A Scout is COURTEOUS. A Scout is polite to everyone regardless of age or position. He knows that good manners make it easier for people to get along together.

A Scout is KIND. A Scout understands there is strength in being gentle. He treats others as he wants to be treated. Without good reason, he does not harm or kill any living thing.

A Scout is OBEDIENT. A Scout follows the rules of his family, school, religion, and troop. He obeys the laws of his community and country. If he thinks these rules and laws are unfair, he tries to have them changed in an orderly manner rather than disobey them.

A Scout is CHEERFUL. A Scout looks for the bright side of life. He cheerfully does tasks that come his way. He tries to make others happy.

A Scout is THRIFTY. A Scout works to pay his way and to help others. He saves for the future. He protects and conserves natural resources. He carefully uses time and property.

Methods of Scouting

A Scout is BRAVE. A Scout can face danger even if he is afraid. He has the courage to stand for what he thinks is right even if others laugh at him or threaten him.

A Scout is CLEAN. A Scout keeps his body and mind fit and clean. He chooses the company of those who live by these same ideals. He helps keep his home and community clean.

A Scout is REVERENT. A Scout is reverent toward God. He is faithful in his religious duties. He respects the beliefs of others.

Special attention must be given to the 12th point of the Scout Law: A scout is Reverent. Often times pronounced "A scout is reverend" by new initiates in the Scouting way. Boy Scouting never teaches or advocates that boys in the program adhere to any particular religious doctrine. It does insist that every boy have a reverence for a higher power. How one in their own home and in their own heart defines that term is totally their choice.

What is important is that every child comes to see, accept, and hopefully experience the divine in themself, in their leaders and fellow scouts, and ultimately all things around them. If we teach young men about the divine through what they experience in wilderness, in community, and in self, they will gain a better appreciation for religious thought, principle,

and practice. Often we find that many have never prayed or
even engaged in a single in-depth discussion about the divine.]

3. PATROLS

During manhood training, boys are broken up into small
groups of five. In Scouting this is called the patrol method.
This group becomes a community that is responsible for its
own housing, food, and general well-being. Boys in the groups
are assigned responsibilities that contribute to the better
function of the patrol. The patrol's success depends on
cooperation and effective leadership. Every child is given an
opportunity to lead.

In the patrol method, boys are taught to share loads.
For a patrol style camp-out, one boy will carry a tent for two
while another will carry the food. A third might carry the
cookware, and others will carry other camping necessities. This
miniature community of boys is being taught teamwork and
rudimentary forms of communal living.

Additionally, teaching youth in smaller groups is more
effective when providing explanations and demonstrations of
new skills. And small groups are much more manageable for
adult leaders. This 1-to-5 ratio of adult to boys allows for
more one-on-one counseling as well as the development of

the skills of young leaders. When given just enough people to be responsible for, they are not overwhelmed by the experience or daunted in mastering leadership techniques when working with so many varying personalities.

4. OUTDOORS

The sight of animals as strays in the street or behind glass and bars will never compare to the awe and wonderment stirred by the first sight of a small lizard scurrying by or the quiet roar of a million creatures under a starlit sky. Such moments help to put life in perspective for youth. Used properly, they allow for truly insightful discussion. They send the false bravado that so many of our boys exhibit today scurrying back to the tent like that lizard moments earlier, leaving only a curious child seeking answers to his questions from caring adults. We as leaders should seek to meet young people there. Many of the skills being taught and the ideals being learned can be discussed and demonstrated most effectively in these moments.

1) Service to others through conservation projects;
2) Fitness through high-adventure activities;
3) Cooperation through sharing responsibilities;
4) Self-reliance through meal planning and camp preparation; and
5) Learning by doing.

More importantly, it is one of the surest ways, without a crisis as a catalyst, to bring a person into a greater awareness of the limitations of their power. You cannot hide behind walls of brick and stone and sincerely laud the works of the divine.

5. ADVANCEMENT

The advancement component is expressly designed for use as a careful measure of a boy's success in Scouting. It's also the surest way to recognize a youngster for his time and effort. It is important that a boy receives his badges with some fanfare, much the same as when trophies are awarded. Clear requirements are outlined for Scouts to earn various merit badges. The advancement component allows Scouts to work alone and in groups to complete tasks and badge work. As the boy completes each badge, he advances through the ranks of Scouting from Scout to Tenderfoot 2nd Class, to 1st Class, to Star Scout, to Life Scout, until he reaches the highest rank: Eagle Scout.

Not typical of other programs and sports, Scouting emphasizes cooperation over competition. Advancement and other activities very often require Scouts to assist each other. To earn the rank of Eagle, a Scout must recruit the aid of other Scouts for his project's completion, without exception.

41

Methods of Scouting

Success is usually group driven, and most events and activities culminate with personal success and victories.

Merit badges all require some writing and reading as well as mastery of hands-on skills. The range of merit badges is broad and diverse, from art to zoology, the sciences, athletics, communications, history, etc., the list goes on and on.

A counselor must be consulted for each merit badge taken. This reinforces interaction with adults. These sessions are usually conducted in small groups with Scouts specifically interested in a particular badge. This minimizes discipline concerns for lack of interest. It also encourages the Scouts to complete the coursework quickly.

6. ADULT ASSOCIATION

"The rise of homes headed by single mothers means that more and more boys have to go through the most formative years with little or no positive adult male role modeling."
—Kim Sexton-Lewter, Health
Educator, UNC-Greensboro

The role of Scout Leader requires strength, knowledge, and honesty. As your Scouting program progresses, you will learn more about the kids in your care—their families and the life circumstances that they face. Your time with them will be as much about who they are and who they are becoming as what new Scout skills they're learning. This is a crux for any youth program. It's crucial to be able to listen and when necessary share your own experiences in a positive and educational way.

Unfortunately, positive role modeling is what black boys are getting least of today. So much of what they know of black manhood is caricature. Media images and the bravado of contemporaries, who also have little real male role modeling, lead to and perpetuate the caricature.

7. PERSONAL GROWTH

We should not teach our children to live their lives with the expectation that they will experience no hardships or suffering. Rather we should work to make sure that what they learn makes them capable of handling adversity when it comes. Such is the path of a warrior...

"The path of a warrior is not an easy one. Warriors make mistakes, feel pain, get scared, and they cry. Sometimes they fight with themselves. All of this doesn't matter because warriors keep going in spite of it all, in spite of themselves. They persist in fighting to become the person they desperately

need to be; a better person for the Creator, for their family, friends, community, coworkers, clients, and themselves. Warriors are people like you—and like me." (D.J. Vanas, 2003)

We are all warriors in life. We are all fighting to find ourselves, to become the person we believe our Creator intended us to be. Our development and growth as individuals hinges on many factors. One of them is the will to face life. Our will develops as we build confidence. Our confidence comes as we realize successes and survive failures. When we assess our strengths and weaknesses, our faith grows in our ability to face life's challenges.

The truth is we are all fragile creatures. Not in the sense that we are weak. Quite the contrary, we are finely tuned instruments designed to shine the brightest light and to reverberate with the most harmonious sound. Black boys, especially, are not being taught this truth about themselves. Instead they are being and have been told an incredible lie about who and what they are. It cripples their opinion of themselves and distorts their perceptions of others.

A Scout, much like a warrior, is seeking to know himself. His personal growth depends, in part, on his classroom and his teachers. When we are taught by good teachers that we have within us all that we need to achieve our goals and to manifest our gifts and talents, we strive to prove them right. When we are not taught this, we learn to take the gifts of others and envy their talent. Scouting provides the classroom for good teachers to help boys discover and develop their own gifts and talents.

8. LEADERSHIP DEVELOPMENT

Leaders are not born, they are cultivated. Leadership is not a talent in and of itself. It is more akin to a blunt piece of metal that needs to be sharpened and honed to a fine edge. Certainly 99 percent of any knife is metal. But what makes it a knife is the blade. So it is with leadership. In truth, holding a title or position of authority is a major component of being a leader. But being able to lead is vastly more important than titles.

Being able to lead means you are aware of your followers' needs. You have a vision and you recognize the value of corralling resources for a specific goal or activity. In Scouting, leadership development is accomplished through a number of methods. Here are four examples:

1) The Boy Scout troop and patrol method gives every boy an opportunity to lead in his patrol or troop. Older Scouts

are typically responsible for teaching basic skills and providing direction for younger members.

2) Community service and Eagle projects require a boy to organize and lead other Scouts to accomplish a specific task.

3) The troop has several (rotating) positions of leadership that every boy is required to fulfill.

4) During camp-outs, hikes, and other outings, boys are expected to assume different positions and responsibilities.

9. UNIFORM

The great equalizer, uniforms, gives each boy that wears one an instant sense of belonging, identity, and purpose. Boys are taught from early on to be honorable and to have something to fight for: family, neighborhood, self-respect. The uniform is a public declaration of how they see themselves. It is also a spokesperson for the wearer's accomplishments. Badges and patches show achievements without bragging.

WHY A SINGLE SEX PROGRAM

Many continue to argue against the Scouting program because of its boys' only policy. However, there are legitimate reasons for providing a single-sex learning environment for boys and girls. The efficacy of single-sex instructional settings has been well established by modern science and has been practiced in African, as well as other, cultures for thousands of years. Research shows that boys and girls do in fact learn differently. While no racial/ethnic differences can be found when looking at the brain, there are significant differences found when observing the brain in relation to gender. These differences translate into how girls and boys receive and process information. One example is found in how girls, as opposed to boys, use language:

"When noted linguist and Georgetown University professor Deborah Tannen compared how girls and boys of different ages use language, she was overwhelmed by the difference that separated the females at each age, and the striking similarities that linked the females, on one hand, and the males, on the other, across the vast expanse of age. In many ways, the second-grade girls were more like the 25-year-old women than like the second-grade boys." (Sax, 2004)

Why a Single Sex Program

Understanding how boys learn is a priority for anyone attempting to educate, instruct, and support their positive growth and development. Recent studies reflect the growing trend in urban centers across the nation. More and more public schools are establishing single-sex public schools for black boys living in disparaging socioeconomic conditions. The results are increasingly positive and prove to have long-term benefits for boys and girls in these educational settings. Evidence shows lasting improvements in grades and test scores, fewer discipline referrals, decreased risk of teenage pregnancy, heightened self-esteem and self-image for boys and girls.

It should be noted that peer pressure is one of the first causes, reasons, or excuses children and their adult caregivers offer for the negative behaviors and attitudes youth demonstrate. What appears understated in this line of reasoning is the impact of peer pressure involving coed relationships. Beyond the pressure to become sexually active, there is the hypersensitive concern about one's appearance, reputation, and social status. In structured single-sex environments this kind of pressure is profoundly reduced. In Scouting, for boys or girls, the single-sex program coupled with a uniform dress code succeeds in increasing learning and reducing social and material distractions.

SCOUTING: CULTURE & PERCEPTION

**No idea is more powerful or relevant
than the one you have about yourself.**

Scouting is very much a class/cultural experience. Scouting is designed for all youth but bears the mark and stamp of middle-class values. This is an inescapable fact. What is offered and learned, however, is for all youth irrespective of race, class, or religion. Scouting offers a kind of cultural capital that will enable them to take advantage of opportunities in the future.

Scouting: Culture & Perception

"...Cultural capital is acquired through family life, formal education, informal educational experiences such as visiting museums and zoos, social connections, networks, friendships, proficiency with cultural codes and nuances, and community.... The point here is that individuals inherit different opportunities for cultural capital, and lack of cultural capital can pose a significant impediment for advancement." *(Shapiro, 2004)*

Scouting offers a relatively loose knit sense of fraternity among Scouters, which can open doors in business and higher education. The broad range of activities a Scout experiences strengthens vocabulary and conversational knowledge. Most Scouts can talk about everything from Indian rituals and lore to boats, climbing gear, and the intricacies of government. The range is so broad, so diverse it contributes to awareness and language ability.

"Cultural capital is yet another form of inheritance that allows families with ample assets to pass along non-monetary benefits to their children that give them a competitive edge in school, the job market, and other areas." *(Shapiro, 2004)*

All these experiences—the hands-on learning, the introduction of common and uncommon tools, materials and equipment, and the value-emphasis education—make Scouts better prepared and more capable at an earlier age relative to their non-Scout peers. These advantages, both tangible and intangible, help produce thinking, healthy minds that engender confident youngsters who see themselves as capable achievers taking on tasks and challenges willingly.

"It's more than the absence of risk, it's the presence of opportunities.... Put simply, while some children score -1(risk factor) and others 0 (absence of risk), a third scores +1(an opportunity factor). The goal . . . is not just to reduce risk; the goal is to help all children to be in the +1 group" *(Garbarino, 1995)*

SAT tests, job interviews, college applications all reflect the dominant sociocultural value system. It is the language spoken and unspoken. While the African American community across every economic class has its own forms of cultural expression, what we think of as white middle class cultural expression and values act as the customary standard for the greater society. Essentially, in societal terms this is the meeting ground for formal communication and social activity.

Negative perceptions of the aptitude of black boys are wrongly derived from standards reflective of culture and class, not intelligence. Knowing that, it still remains vital that members of any non-dominant culture and/or class become not only aware but savvy in their knowledge of dominant sociocultural values and expressions. In short, anything less limits one's "cultural capital" and can hinder advancement.

Scouting: Culture & Perception

Perceptions, Perceptions, Perceptions

In the 1960s the Scouting movement's growth in the black community stagnated. The new political consciousness of the civil rights era caused blacks to push Scouting out because of its patriotic ethos. In like fashion, whites pulled out, the few who were there, with equal fervor.

Between the first and second World Wars, Scouting slowly grew in the North and Midwest in the black community. Even though some saw it as an excellent tool for youth development, many more identified boys in uniforms as an effort to prepare kids for military service and steered their sons away. Probably, the most significant catalyst to spur African American growth and interest in Scouting was the veterans return to the community after the World War II.

The respect and honor attributed to these men despite the racism and disrespect they faced from the greater society, their knowledge and outdoor skills, all contributed to growth in organizing Scout units. It's also likely that the many rural-born blacks who moved to urban centers did not lose their love for the outdoors, fishing, hunting, whittling, etc.

These returning veterans in uniform, with fascinating stories and camping skills, coupled with transplants from the Deep South, fresh off the farm, could have been a major reason for the program's acceptance. The dignity of the uniform and the veterans' collective experiences had to have impacted the psyches of young boys and their families. Not only did they want the same respect and pride afforded the soldiers but also there was suddenly an abundance of men capable of teaching youngsters about the outdoors and basic survival.

Research shows that people well respected in the community held the position of Scoutmaster. Typically they were doctors, school principals, educators, professionals, and locally renowned people.

Scoutreach

This is the outreach effort of the national office of the BSA to see that Scouting is afforded every child in every community in the country. If you intend to serve low-income youth of any ethnic/religious origin and support for the program will be a challenge, contact the local Boy Scouts council to inquire about resources for support.

Scoutreach units are very often led by paid adult leaders. Staff of the local council are hired and trained to increase awareness of Scout programs in hard-to-serve communities and to provide a quality Scouting program. If you are able to organize a Scoutreach unit, do support their activities as a committee member or leader. Hard-to-serve communities are just that, hard to serve. Any support you can provide is sorely needed.

Senior Scouts teaching younger boys reinforces learning and builds peer trust.

The local fire department is an excellent resource for teaching basic Scout skills.

RUNNING A SCOUT TROOP

Getting Started

It's vital to get boys into the program at an early age. It's important for black boys to be inducted before their minds have been trained to fear and resent adult black males. Boys need to be reached by 7 years of age. Ideally, 11 years old is the optimum age to begin an intense, focused approach. Scout troops begin registering boys at 10 1/2-11 years of age.

At this age, most boys enjoy outdoor activities and learning and exploring new things. Camping is always an experience boys wonder about. Other activities include fishing, hikes, nature walks, etc. Few youth show absolutely no interest in outdoor activities.

For adults, learning to camp is by no means as difficult as it may seem, and a lot can be learned by simply reading a book. The guides, training, and materials offered by local Scout councils can provide even the novice with a good start. It is okay and even important to make mistakes in front of the boys in your charge. It provides the youth with an opportunity to learn in a more participatory fashion. It is also a means to determine if kids are learning what is being taught.

Running a Scout Troop

Most youth in their first camp-out will be excited and intimidated. It is important to set strict guidelines, rules, and parameters for what is acceptable camp behavior. Clear rules and expectations coupled with the fear of the unknown can curtail the excitement in order to maintain a safe and productive camp-out. Make it a point to ban all electronic devices. They can listen to radios, CDs, MP3s, and play Gameboys™ at home. The Scouts are camping out to experience something new and different. Being uncomfortable and vulnerable to that which is new is par for the course.

If you have a group that is a "handful," you'll want to arrive at camp late in the day, right at dusk or early evening, depending on how experienced your young campers are. If they've never put a tent up before, a late start on departure day will make the completion of that task that much more important. They will pay greater attention to your instructions when the alternative is to sleep outside, unsheltered. You'll have more control and less trouble. If you have experienced campers, time of day won't really matter, and very early starts might be in order, with a full day of chores and tasks to be completed.

Whatever you've learned, practiced, and taught in your meetings needs to be tested in the outdoors. As the adult leader, you should take every opportunity to have the boys do the work, with exceptions being that which is absolutely necessary, dangerous, or difficult. This is a boy-run operation. You are working to develop men from boys, not entertain them.

The boys will often fail. The leader's goal is not to keep them from failing and certainly not to berate them for failure. Rather a boy's failure is an opportunity for lesson teaching. For the more headstrong, the only opportunity you have to teach them anything may occur in the midst of their failure. These know-it-alls really learn best when they realize they don't know it all. The problem with know-it-alls is they soon forget. Adults who lead like know-it-alls are in danger of losing credibility with the youth in their care when they fail or make mistakes, as they inevitably will.

Be honest. What you don't know you can learn. The goal is not to feign superior strength and wisdom. The goal is to make it possible for the group of boys to grow in moral strength and knowledge.

Applying Knowledge

Scouting's most vital gift is its demonstrated use of practical knowledge, that is, applied skills. Next to learning to read and write, basic first aid, principles of survival and conservation, use of natural surroundings (awareness)—this kind of knowledge is tangible. It enables a young man to develop self-confidence and greater self-sufficiency. Those men and women who have survived and have even been successful without any substantial education usually have managed to do well because of their mastery and awareness of practical knowledge. Actually, for thousands of years well before the advent of reading and writing, this was the only knowledge that mattered: being able to take care of yourself and your community.

When you burned yourself and grandma quickly, calmly rubbed cocoa butter on it, putting your fear to rest while at the same time easing your pain, she demonstrated the power of applied knowledge. Because of what she knew and how well she knew it, she was able to take control of the situation and rescue you from your own pain and fear.

What she demonstrated was less from academic knowledge and more from applied, time-tested experience. It can't be taken away, and it is as vital as any book or arithmetic lesson.

Tying Knots

The simple skill of knot tying, the learning of different knots for various needs, contributes to a young man's ability to master a skill that he can use, demonstrate, and share. This skill most likely will be taken for granted, initially. But when a boy masters this skill, and others, he will learn to appreciate his new ability. Why? Because we all encounter a need to use rope, string, etc., at some point in time. Whether it's to help someone move, tie down a piece of luggage, or simply hold an object in place, everyone needs to be able to fasten, hold, brace, or connect using a knot. The square knot is the first knot taught to Boy Scouts.

In Scouting the square not symbolizes unity. Its principal function is to connect two ropes together. The more stress you apply, the better the knot holds. Yet it can be undone with little effort when the tension is released. It is a simple knot to learn and makes the learning of more complicated knots tenable.

Knot tying requires patience and implies a certain level of handiness. Nothing frustrates a Scout, child, or adult more than to forget or not know the best knot for the job and how it's tied. In truth, though it may not be absolutely vital to our existence knot tying does offer a great deal in the way of developing a boy's hand-eye coordination, dexterity, problem-solving skills, and most of all, his confidence. Knot tying should be a part of every public school curriculum.

Running a Scout Troop

Cultivating Free & Independent Thought

"The more students work at storing the deposits entrusted to them, the less they develop the critical consciousness which would result from their intervention in the world as transformers of that world. The more completely they accept the passive role imposed on them, the more they tend simply to adapt to the world as it is and to the fragmented view of reality deposited in them." (Freire, 1970)

The purpose of this book is not to "train" our youth. It is to enable them to live without needing to be trained. Being able to think for oneself requires that you (1) develop your power to perceive critically the way you exist in the world in which you find yourself; and (2) have the freedom to interpret life through your own lens of experience and consciousness. Ideally, Scouting accepts boys as conscious beings with their own way of seeing. To sustain that ideal, we must recognize that people teach each other. There are right and wrong ways of doing things, but the best experiences are those in which we are both teacher and student. Scout leaders will tell you that Scouts will always learn something new. By putting them in positions to lead and make ethical decisions, we are cultivating free thinkers. Free thinkers are capable of offering creative solutions to community problems, beginning with their own.

WHY SCOUTING WORKS FOR BLACK BOYS

On Manhood

"Black men in this society have not generally been granted traditional masculine privilege or power. Social, cultural, and economic forces manifested in racism and oppression through American history have combined to keep black men from assuming traditionally accepted masculine roles." (Wilson, 1991)

When men do not share definitions for manhood with boys, as women can't do this for boys, boys will define manhood for themselves, based on what they learn from other boys and media. What boys learn about manhood from media images are at best a distortion, at worst a gross perversion that only perpetuates/promotes much of the sociopath-like behaviors in impoverished neighborhoods.

The exaggerated bravado and hypersensitivity to codes of respect and recognition are a direct result of a kind of cultural machismo exacerbated and manipulated by images in film, music, and print. In fact, the exaggerated image has become the cultural norm. Only groups /organizations that tolerate and encourage that image draw young men. Groups like gangs and in some ways organizations such as athletic teams, fraternities, and other social groups when unchecked can attract youth by their machismo rather than their mission.

61

Running a Scout Troop

What you propose as a Scout leader is a different model for manhood. You are, by demonstration, teaching the actual tenets that truly define the difference between being a man and just happening to be male. In place of the use of force and intimidation to get one's way, a Scout leader teaches patience and problem solving. In place of ridicule and disrespect for others, a Scout leader teaches cooperation and the team ethic. In place of body emphasis, a Scout leader emphasizes creativity and mental acuity. He helps boys to identify with the man they are becoming rather than an idolized media image.

Goals, Expectations, Standards & Accountability

High expectations begin the journey. Any learning experience must be approached with the expectation that the journeyman will learn something. It's a truth that manifests itself whether you believe it or not. It is impossible to not learn.

Journey guides, teachers, and adult leaders must engage the participants with the high expectation not only that they will learn but will actually learn something of what you're attempting to teach them if not all of it.

Our biggest failure as a society in general and as a community in particular is that we look at our youth through the eyes of challenge as opposed to opportunity. Consciously and subconsciously we decide that minority youth are a problem we need to fix. Fixing can mean anything from providing entertainment to helping them learn to just keeping them occupied. We are not addressing them or their needs with a vision; we instead, are viewing them through a prism.

Without a vision-standard, an intention to see youth beyond where they are, regardless of where they are, you will at best have mediocre success in helping boys to become better human beings. At worst, you will become jaded and intolerable of youth and their situations. You will blame them. You must have an idea of who they can become, not only in your mind but also in your program and actions.

In Scouting the vision is that every child will become a good Scout, not an Eagle Scout, a good Scout. Why? It's simple: society is built on the will of good men and women. Accomplishing the rank of Eagle is a difficult thing. It is a truth you can verify by looking at the percentage of young men that go on to attain that rank: nationally, less than 2 percent. Those that achieve Eagle Scout are by no means superhuman. It's more likely they are matched with the right leader, in the right troop, at the right time, with just enough desire and parent support to accomplish what is required. Cohering all those factors at the same time is what is great and rare and exceedingly difficult to duplicate.

We place no limits on the distance they can travel. We do impose limits on how they make that journey. The path is straight and narrow. It is not all down hill and easy, but it is not terribly difficult so long as the appropriate resources and supports are in place. Standards include: wearing the uniform when appropriate; reverence for a higher power; boy-run operations, etc.

Goals help boys to appreciate delayed gratification. Goals require work, which usually requires a time commitment. When they see the results of their efforts and recall the process by which they achieved those results, it will be easier for them to subdue the urge for instant gratification and better plan and set goals for themselves in adulthood.

Goals are needed like signs on a road. Goals can be used as a means to an end. The advancement program in Scouting is a clear form of goal measurement. High expectations must be matched with goals. Goals let the Scout know he has accomplished his task or some portion thereof. If a Scout determines or is left to determine his success or failure solely based on your expectations, he will either rebel or become docile if and when he loses interest in meeting that expectation.

Clear goals help to prevent leaders from becoming tyrannical with their authority. The only adults who, if any, need to or are licensed to have expectations for a child without clearly established goals are parents. As parents, we should consider raising our children employing goals in addition to our fleeting and varying expectations.

Expectations are most effective when they are congruent with measurable goals. That is the only way we can retain comparable expectations for every child. If we base our expectations on the charted goals we've set, the Scout or child can make the rational connection.

Lastly, it's important to know the difference between expectations and aspirations and avoid confusing the two. We can aspire to see every boy in our troop earn the rank of Eagle, but we should not live with that as an expectation. However, we should expect that all boys in the troop participate fully, do his fair share, and contribute to the troop experience.

Story Telling

Campfires are excellent venues for the presentation of information. Dancing flames are hypnotic and have a calming effect on people. Engaging youth in conversations, whether in groups or individually, can be quite revealing and also insightful for everyone. Offering wisdom-filled insights through end-of-day reflections, telling stories to entertain or inform, or both, are yet other means of teaching and creating an amazing learning experience for all.

Games, Games, Games!

What is Scouting without games? A Scouting meeting must be filled with activities— games and events that are fun will involve and invigorate the bonding and growing process. Games attract and keep the attention of Scout youth. Without them you have a lecture series. There are moments when talking or formal instruction is unavoidable, even necessary. But the instruction is why the boy's parents signed them up. It's not why the boy joined. While you are not there solely to entertain, you are encouraged to provide what is called "edutainment."

A Scout leader must accomplish two things right away: esprit de corps and some mastery of basic skills. This depends heavily on what takes place in your meetings. Games and activities build team mentality, foster competitive spirit, teach basic skills, and strengthen commitment to the troop while being—most importantly—fun. All of the positive elements are disguised in the fun. The fun is what will be most remembered. The lessons learned, the skills mastered may or may not be applied in the future. Yet if these events are not fun, it's almost certain that they won't be applied in the future or retained beyond the present.

Games are also effective means for determining attitudes, behaviors, strengths, and weaknesses of the youth. Puzzle games might be difficult and frustrating, testing their will to endure and stick to a difficult task. Physical games may test athletic ability, physical stamina, and constitution. Games of skill test dexterity, motor skills, flexibility, and discipline. As you instruct , you'll identify and learn the weaknesses and strengths of your charges. You won't have to record what you see; your awareness will just happen as you grow more familiar with the boys.

Games are used in outdoor programs to develop teamwork and team mentality among participants. Project C.O.P.E. (Challenging Outdoor Personal Experience) is a high-adventure program developed by the BSA that focuses directly on group development and leadership skills, using initiative games and high-ropes courses.

Community Service

"Social scientists describe high-risk neighborhoods as 'an ecological conspiracy against children.'" (Werner & Smith 1992)

Running a Scout Troop

Any form of community service is probably the most empowering practice a Scout unit can do. Here is where the importance of giving becomes manifest, and the reality of what a community is becomes tangible. So many children grow up in cities and in neighborhoods and households that are dangerous and even hostile to their existence. It is virtually impossible to convince any person to assist someone or something that seeks to harm them or refuses to help them in their own time of need. It is vital that we turn that perception around. Through service projects and other efforts to assist people in need, Scouts can become aware of their power and ability to help others. The translation: If a person can make life better for others, he or she can make life better for themself.

Camping

Camping is the reason for the Scout program. It is the reason why boys join the Boy Scouts. The allure of the out doors, the opportunity to test their own mettle and challenge their own fears are why boys join and why they come. Camping is one of the most effective means at our disposal to reach boys. The out of doors is a classroom of sorts. It makes the instruction real to the students. It offers the epitome of learning by doing. Virtually everything about the out of doors is taught by demonstration, practice, and performance. All out of doors activities—hikes, nature trails, games, sports, campfires, and overnighters—can be used to teach respect, responsibility, resourcefulness, fitness, faith, perseverance, and honesty.

On Being Prepared

Prepare for meetings, activities, and camp-outs. The format for Scout meetings is laid out in several Scout books, handouts at trainings, etc. Follow the format. Remain consistent, and don't deviate unless necessary. The purpose of Scouting is to let the boys run the show. This is a "boy-run" operation. Establish a format and a pattern they can follow. If you open with prayer, always open with prayer. If the Pledge of Allegiance or the Scout Oath follows, then don't change. Make the order important. It makes the meeting easier for you and for the boys. Once they can run the protocol, it will free you up to better prepare for the meat of the meeting.

Training

BSA provides a number of training and skills courses to help volunteer leaders better grasp the Scouting program. From the Outdoor Leader Skills course to the highest training course for adults, Wood Badge, every class is taught in both the classroom and the outdoors, much the same way a typical Scouting program operates.

Running a Scout Troop

Parents

Unfortunately, some parents don't recognize the value of the program or their role in its success. Don't turn away or punish boys by exclusion solely because their parent(s) doesn't support the troop. However, since so few parents in the black community have been introduced to Scouting in any kind of meaningful way, they may be reluctant to participate.

It's the leader's responsibility to get gradual support by asking parents to do small tasks. As the tasks are accomplished, the parents will become receptive to doing more. Be warned, this is a process with ebbs and flows. Some parents will never move past baking a cake or decorating a room for a ceremony. That's fine. Plan your calendar so that there are ample opportunities for them to do these things year round.

Unlike sports where parents can sit on the sidelines while their child participates, Scouting depends on some parental involvement. Parents have to do more because their children are asked to do more, in most cases.

Flying Solo

There are, on occasion, times when the Scoutmaster is without the support of adults who have assumed volunteer roles in the troop. The Scoutmaster may even be without an Assistant Scoutmaster. This less than ideal situation is particularly common for Scout troops in fragile neighborhoods. Nevertheless, as the unit leader, there are practices you can implement to sustain your troop program.

The first step is to contact a representative of the chartered organization. This would typically be an executive officer, director or leader of office, church or organization where your meetings are held. It is the responsibility of the chartering institution to provide volunteer leadership to the troop. If this doesn't prove fruitful right away there are some other ways to continue your program.

Unless you have the required two-deep leadership, you will have to rule out camp-outs and field trips. As for meetings, if you meet in a school, Boys & Girls Club, church, or other place where adults, such as staff or volunteers not affiliated with the troop, are present, you can ask them to keep a visible presence at the meetings.

Certainly, parents that have not been involved can support your efforts on a meeting-by-meeting basis. You don't have to ask for long-term attendance if they are unable or unwilling. Direct phone calls, stating a need, are effective with all but the most disinterested or inaccessible of parents. Impress upon them your absolute inability to continue without their commitment. Scout siblings 18 and older also qualify. As a last resort, ask friends and/or family. Refer to some of the methods in the next chapter, "Maintaining Your Troop," as well.

MAINTAINING YOUR TROOP

If you are already running a troop or Scouting program, here are some things you can do to promote interest and excitement about Scouting.

1. Introduce athletics: basketball tournaments, golf clinics, etc.

2. Make greater use of council resources: COPE program, climbing tower.

3. Councils with Scoutreach programs often have camping equipment and supplies available to ease financial burden of individual Scouts and families.

4. Be more creative with class B dress uniform: substitute military khakis, troop T-shirts, different types of hats.

5. Team up with other troops for outings, activities, competitions, etc.

6. Provide off-the-mark trips: consider non-Scouting trips to theaters, movies, sports, go-carts, horse riding tours.

Maintaining Your Troop

7. Introduce outside support, contact corporations and small businesses to fund/ offset cost of more expensive outings.

8. Call all of your friends: get other adult males involved— boys are drawn to adult males.

9. Don't always use the patrol method for meals: cook large feasts; people return for good food and fun.

10. Get trained! The better trained you are the more confident and resourceful you'll be as a leader or committee member.

THE CHARGE

"Gentlemen of the jury, look at this—this—this boy. I almost said man, but I can't say man. Oh, sure, he has reached the age of 21, when we, civilized men, consider the male species has reached manhood, but would you call this—this— this a man? No not I. I would call it a boy and a fool. A fool does what others tell him to do." (Gaines, 1993)

What are the boys in our community becoming? They are male, but are they growing into men? A male that behaves like a child is still a boy, and a man that thinks and acts like a boy is a fool. When more males are growing up incapable of working together, lacking the skills and ability to take care of themselves, and showing contempt for responsibility and duty to family to the extent that death by homicide and disease are their primary killers and 70 percent of black children are being raised in homes without fathers, you have a community in crisis. The solution to this crisis lies in the crisis itself.

Men are needed in the African American community— men with compassion and commitment that are seeking the tools necessary to engineer change in their community. Scouting is such a tool. Just a few committed adults with a tool such as Scouting can positively impact these young men to help them grow into the solution we seek.

The Charge

This book was written for those who believe all people are divine in nature. This divinity precedes and presupposes environmental risks and upbringing. And because of the inherent nature of our divinity, we are all redeemable. Our children are clearly convinced they are anything but divine, evidenced by their actions and their responses to what life offers them. This is easily apparent from the rising gang involvement and criminal behavior coupled with the sundry other social evils they find themselves ensnared by, i.e., teen pregnancy, drug use, gangs, etc.

Our purpose is to foster and facilitate change in our communities through youth development. But we need a collective transformation. Much talk is made of how important it is to save even a single life, but to save the life of an entire community, a collective change is needed. And a collective change can only come by a concentrated effort of the many on the many.

If every boy in a single housing community were fully engaged in the Scouting program for three years, we would have a positive impact. You could help inculcate an entire generation with like values and at the same time remove the opportunity for transmission of negative values through peers. Maybe it's a crazy concept, but with your help it could work. Please try it.

Appendix A— MERIT BADGES

Agribusiness

American Business

American Culture

American Heritage

American Labor

Animal Science

Archaeology

Archery

Architecture

Art

Astronomy

Athletics

Atomic Energy

Aviation

Backpacking

Basketry

Beekeeping

Bird Study

Botany

Bugling

Camping

Canoeing

Chemistry

Cinematography

Citizenship of the Community

Citizenship of the Nation

Citizenship of the World Coin

Buying

Coin Collection

Communications

Computers

Cooking

Crime Prevention

Cycling

Dentistry

Disabilities Awareness

Dog Care

Drafting

Electricity

Electronics

Emergency Preparedness

Energy

Engineering

Entrepreneurship

Environmental Science Family

Life

Appendix

Farm Mechanics

Fingerprinting

Fire Safety

First Aid

Fish & Wildlife Management

Fishing

Fly Fishing

Forestry

Gardening

Genealogy

General Science

Geology

Golf

Graphic Arts

Hiking

Home Repair

Horsemanship

Indian Lore

Insect Study

Journalism

Landscape Architecture

Law

Leather

Lifesaving

Machinery

Mammal Study

Masonry

Metalwork

Model Design and Building

Motorboating

Music

Nature

Oceanography

Orienteering

Painting

Personal Fitness

Personal Management

Pets

Photography

Pioneering

Plant Science

Plumbing

Pottery

Public Health

Public Speaking

Pulp & Paper

Rabbit Raising

Radio

Railroading

Reading

Reptile Study

Rifle Shooting

Rowing

Safety

Salesmanship

Scholarship

Sculpture

Shotgun Shooting

Signaling

Skating

Small Boat Sailing

Soil and Water Conservation

Space Exploration

Sports

Stamp Collecting

Surveying

Swimming

Textiles

Theater

Traffic Safety

Truck Transportation

Veterinary Medicine

Waterskiing

Weather

Whitewater Rafting

Wilderness Survival

Woodcarving

Woodwork

Appendix B—LITERATURE
& RESOURCES

Challenging Games

Field Book

Program Features volumes I,
II, & III

Scout Handbook

Scoutmaster's Manual

Appendix

Appendix C—AFRICAN ORIGINS OF SCOUTING

<u>Kudu Horn</u>: The kudu is one of the largest species of antelope in Africa, noted for the two long spiraling horns that grow from the top of its head. These magnificent horns were hollowed out by the Matabele and used as a means to signal over distances during their resistance to the British. It is said that in victory, Lord Baden Powell took as a spoil the Kudu horn held by an officer in the Matabele army. This Kudu horn was used by Powell to signal the opening of the first Scout camp at Brownsea Island in 1907.

<u>Pioneering</u>: Making a way out of no way. Many of the simple techniques of knot tying, uses for rope, a knife, an axe, and other tools are derived from the pioneering work done during the different military campaigns waged by the British in Africa. Creating roads, paths, and bridges required ingenuity and hard work. The Africans enlisted to prepare a way for the British troops were skilled in these techniques and demonstrated how the environment offered everything necessary. Today, in Scouting the learning and mastery of these techniques can be summed up in the Scout motto: Be Prepared.

<u>Scout Handshake</u>: Scouts shake with the left hand. This is adapted from an Ashanti warrior custom to which is attributed the saying, "Only the bravest of the brave shake with the left

hand." A warrior's left arm is his shield-bearing arm. To lay down your shield while your enemy still possessed his weapon in his right hand was a sign of a warrior's courage.

Scout Staff: When camping, Scouts are taught the many uses of a walking stick. A long, strong, lightweight staff has many uses when hiking, backpacking, or traveling in woodlands, mountains, or wilderness terrain. The Scout staff was adapted from the work done during the Ashanti campaign led by Lord Baden Powell. Because of the nature of the campaign, most of the reconnaissance had to be done at night through dense jungle. These early recon patrols were made up of many different warriors, and most were enemies of the Ashanti. The Scout staff was a tool integral to the success of these military expeditions. It was used to navigate over unpredictable terrain and through the darkness, as well as assist with clearing roads, testing stream depths, etc., as they built bridges and cleared paths over which the British soldiers could move.

Wood Badge Beads: Today, at the conclusion of an advanced leader training program known as Wood Badge, graduates are given two wooden beads tied together by a leather string. They symbolize the successful completion of Scouting's most prestigious training courses for adults. These beads are identical to the beads worn as ornamentation by Dinizulu, leader of a Zulu rebellion against British annexation,

Appendix

who was defeated by Powell. Upon the Zulu's defeat, it is alleged that Lord Powell was either given the beads by Dinizulu or they were retrieved from Dinizulu's body. As early as 1825, eyewitness accounts report such beads being worn by Shaka Zulu who personally distributed them as recognition to Zulu warriors. Powell gave replicas of these very same beads to leaders who had completed adult leader training under his tutelage in the early years of the Scouting movement.

Appendix D—ADDITIONAL SCOUTING PRACTICES

SCOUT SIGN & SALUTE

The Scout sign marks you as a Scout everywhere in the world. Give it each time you recite the Scout Oath and Law. Held high, the Scout sign is a signal for attention. When a Scout leader raises his hand in the Scout sign, all Scouts should also make the sign and come to silent attention. To give the Scout sign, cover the nail of the little finger on your right hand with your right thumb. Then raise your right hand, palm forward, with the three middle fingers extended upward. Those three fingers stand for the three parts of the Scout Oath. Your thumb and little finger touch to represent the bond that unites all Scouts.

The Scout Salute is made with the same hand sign placed at a slight angle above the right eye.

SCOUT MOTTO

Be Prepared. The Scout motto sums up the special purpose of Boy Scouting. Every Scout understands the meaning of the motto from the very first time he repeats it.

SCOUT SLOGAN

Do a Good Turn Daily. In short, Scouts are encouraged to perform random acts of kindness. Every Scout should seek opportunities to assist family, friends, and strangers, where appropriate, without the expectation of compensation of any kind.

SCOUT HANDCLASP (handshake)

Boy Scouts are taught to shake hands with the left hand (see Appendix C, "Scout Handshake").

OUTDOOR CODE

The Outdoor Code is made up of four points. These points act as a guide and remind Scouts to be aware of and responsible for their surroundings. This is a commitment every Scout program makes that they will maintain the natural environment, leaving it better than when they found it. The "Leave No Trace" ethic is attributed to the practice of the African scout patrols used in the British military campaigns in

Appendix

South Africa. They navigated the tropical terrain, locating the minutest details that told the size, time, and movement of the enemy without revealing their own whereabouts.

As an American, I will do my best to –
Be clean in my outdoor manners,
Be careful with fire,
Be considerate in the outdoors,
And
Be conservation minded.

RESOURCES

Birkby, Robert (1990). *The Boy Scout Handbook*. Irving, Texas: Boy Scouts of America.

Freire, P. (1970). *Pedagogy of the Oppressed*. New York: The Continuum International Publishing Group.

Gaines, E. J. (1993). *A Lesson Before Dying*. New York: Vintage Books.

Garbarino, J. (1995). *Raising Children in a Socially Toxic Environment*. San Francisco: Jossey-Bass.

Louis Harris & Associates (1998). *A Year in the Life of a Cub Scout.... Boy Scout ...Venturer*. Irving, Texas: Boy Scouts of America.

Sax, L. (2004). *Letter to the Office of Civil Rights in the United States Department of Education*. Poolesville, Maryland: National Association for Single Sex Public Education.

Schorr, L. (1989). *Within Our Reach: Breaking the Cycle of Disadvantage*. New York: Doubleday.

Resources

Seton, E. (1911). *The Official Handbook for Boys*. Irving, Texas: Boy Scouts of America.

Shapiro, T. (2004). *The Hidden Cost of Being African-American*. New York: Oxford University Press.

Vanas, D. J. (2003). *The Tiny Warrior: A Path to Personal Discovery and Achievement*. Kansas City, Kansas: Andrews McMeel Publishing.

Washington, M. M. (June 2005). *Pre K Black Kids Are Twice As Likely to Be Expelled*. Wilmington, North Carolina: Greater Diversity News.

Werner, E. E., & Smith, R. S. (1992). *Overcoming the Odds: High Risk Children from Birth to Adulthood*. Ithaca, New York: Cornell University Press.

Wilson, A. (1991). *Understanding Black Adolescent Male Violence: Its Remediation and Prevention*. New York: Afrikan World InfoSystems.